Getting Out Alive

The Autumn Veatch Story

Written by

TARA ELLIS

As told by

AUTUMN VEATCH

Photograph copyrights for:

Image 1. Autumn Veatch, 2,3,4. Tara Ellis Photography 5. Chelsey Clark, 6. Chelsey Clark, 7. Sara Esperance

ISBN-13: 978-1523399918
ISBN-10: 1523399910

Tara Ellis Publications
2015

Getting Out Alive

-The Autumn Veatch Story

Preface

This is a true account of the fatal plane crash that occurred on July 11, 2015, in the Northern Cascade Mountains in Washington State. Autumn Veatch was the only survivor. This is her story, as told by her to author Tara Ellis. It has been written and published with her consent and parental approval.

1.This is a self portrait Autumn took that day and sent to a friend, not long before the crash.

1

Saturday, July 11th, 2015

Approx. 3:20 pm, PST

Sixteen-year-old Autumn Veatch gripped the back of the seat in front of her as the small plane bounced in the turbulence. It was the first time she'd ever been on a small plane, and only her second time flying. Although Autumn hadn't been afraid when she and her grandparents left Kalispell, Montana, a few hours earlier, she was quickly changing her mind.

As the plane settled back into its loud, endless drone, she pried her hands away from where they were clutching the cushion, near her grandfather's shoulders. He was positioned in the pilot's seat, and he turned to smile crookedly at her as she fumbled around, trying to find her phone. The gesture did little to calm her nerves, but she did her best to look composed as she tapped the screen on her phone.

If I die, remember that I love you! She quickly typed, smiling slightly as she sent it to her boyfriend, Newton. Yeah, it was a bit dramatic, but she knew he'd laugh at it. That was the kind of friendship they had, full of wit and sarcasm. She wouldn't want it any other way.

"Are you okay, Autumn?" Looking up at her grandma, Autumn nodded in response. The voice-activated headset she was wearing was a pain to use. With just enough of a delay that it caused them to talk over each other, it made communicating frustrating, so she'd been quiet for most of the trip. It was actually entertaining to listen to the relentless, playful banter between her step-grandparents. That past week, Autumn had gotten to know them pretty well, and she'd been surprised they were so fun to be around. It had been about four years since her mom had married their son, but this trip was the most time she'd ever spent with them.

While the nearly unbearable Montana heat wasn't so horrible in comparison to the constant rain at her home in Bellingham, Washington, she was eager to get back. Newton and his mom were picking her up at the small airport and she couldn't wait to be reunited with her friends. Looking down at the response to her last text, Autumn laughed and tried to forget the tense situation that she was in.

Cloudy weather had delayed their departure that morning until the afternoon, and it was continuing to get worse the closer they got to home. As they flew into the most rugged part of the Northern Cascade Mountains, they lost sight of Hwy 20, the road they were using for navigation.

Now, it was close to 3:30 pm, and it was becoming increasingly obvious that her grandfather wasn't sure where they were. All Autumn could see out the windows were white clouds, and she didn't know where the looming mountains were…hopefully *below* them.

A sudden jerking motion to the right caused her to gasp and look up just in time to see a tree-shrouded cliff disappear behind them! They had almost run straight into it. As her grandparents tried to laugh it off, Autumn fought down her rising panic and turned to her phone, her lifeline, for comfort. However, she saw the undeniable circle with an X through it and groaned at the timing. How could she lose service *now*?

Remembering that her grandma was using her tablet's GPS to help guide them, Autumn wondered if they were totally blind. The thought wasn't reassuring.

"It turned off!" Sharon Bowman cried while frantically pushing at the device. The joking between the older couple just moments ago forgotten, Leland looked at his wife in disbelief.

"You turned it *off*?" His voice was muffled through her headset, but Autumn's anxiety was intensified. His concern was palpable. They were in real trouble.

"It wasn't on purpose!" Sharon answered, sounding desperate.

"I can't see a thing," Leland mumbled. "I'm going to try and get below this cloud bank."

Her knuckles turning white, Autumn did the only thing

she could think of. Making sure her seatbelt was secured, she then seized the back of the pilot seat again, this time putting her head between her knees. She suffered from anxiety on a *good* day, and this was far from being a good day. Eyes squeezed shut, she told herself that they had everything under control and that she was worrying over nothing.

"We're getting too low!" her grandpa shouted. His voice was thick with fear, causing Autumn to suffer a fresh wave of apprehension. "We'll have to go above it instead." His voiced echoed through the headset, sounding farther away as Autumn's pulse pounded in her head, muffling her hearing.

The sudden change in altitude made Autumn's stomach drop, and she swallowed against the bile threatening to rise.

This can't be happening! She thought numbly, willing the plane to climb faster. They had to climb faster, they had to—

Her mantra was interrupted by an earsplitting sound that her mind couldn't place. At the same time, trees replaced the white outside the windows. As if in slow motion, one of the wings broke off, and they continued to plummet through the surreal forest, their forward motion slowing with each new assault to the body of the plane.

Autumn watched in shock as first her phone and then her backpack slid almost gently from her lap and disappeared. Everything roared around her as the headset flew off, and then finally…the nightmare ended.

Or so she thought.

2

Saturday, July 11th, 2015

Approx. 3:30 pm, PST

Fire.

Fire rushed towards her from the front of the plane, and the heat was already agonizing. Pushing at the seatbelt, Autumn struggled to get it off. It wouldn't open.

"No, no, no!" she sobbed, clawing at it blindly, her eyes burning from the heat and smoke. Instinct finally took over and she stopped panicking.

Move, or die.

Pushing up in the seat, she slid her legs out of the belt, thankful that it was loose enough for the maneuver. Straining to see, she turned away from the flames, scrambling over wreckage through the only available route and somehow managing to get outside.

Finding herself standing beside the plane, on the same

side she had been sitting, she turned towards the opening where her grandpa was still strapped in the seat. He was alive, but badly hurt. Fire surrounded around him and she could see her grandma in the seat on the other side. She was screaming, and all Autumn could think was that she had to pull Leland out before she could get to Sharon.

Reaching through the opening, she grabbed at his hands, arms, anything she could get a grip on. Pulling with all of her strength, it had no effect.

"You have to get out!" Autumn screamed, her voice hoarse and barely recognizable. "Take the seatbelt off!" Reaching again for him, she was aware of her right hand burning, and her face was hot from the nearby flames licking around the cockpit.

He was mumbling, moaning, but Autumn couldn't make out what he was saying. Sharon's screams took on a new pitch, and then stopped altogether. The fire had consumed her, and knowing that her grandfather was next, she tugged at him even harder, ignoring her own pain.

This can't be happening. It can't be real. None of this is real, Autumn thought, trying to convince herself.

But the nightmare unfolding around her couldn't be denied, and the man she'd come to love and respect stopped moving under her hands. When the smell of her own charred flesh and singed hair broke through her shock, Autumn was finally compelled to move away from the wreckage, the heat physically pushing her back.

Staring in horror at the raging inferno, the whole plane now engulfed, Autumn stumbled over the unforgiving terrain, shaking her head angrily.

"No!" She yelled, the enormity of what just happened beginning to sink in. "No!" Spinning around, all she could think about was getting away from the hell she'd been thrown into.

Sobbing, blinded by her tears, Autumn plunged through the alien landscape. Branches scraped at her arms and legs, and she fell over countless rocks and logs as the ground dropped away at a steep pitch.

"Why did that have to happen to them?" The words were ripped from her throat and echoed back at her. "Why! Why did they have to die!" It wasn't a question, but an accusation. Autumn knew she sounded crazy, but she couldn't stop, and continued to scream uncontrollably. Her words began to run together until she wasn't making any sense, but fear drove her forward. She knew she had to keep moving if she wanted to stay alive.

Her descent rapidly increased until she was forced to reach out and grab at a tree to stop her forward motion. Placing her forehead against the cool bark, Autumn listened to the rapid thumping of her heart. Crinkling her nose at the foul scent of her hand, her heartrate surged faster at the evidence of what she was fleeing.

"It's not far enough," she whispered at the tree, not expecting an answer. Looking over her shoulder, eyes wide, Autumn touched the scorched edges of her hair with her good left hand, and the cold emptiness of terror threatened to overwhelm her. She had to get away.

Pushing back from the cedar, she continued her flight.

The mountains were timeless. After listening to the pounding of her feet and own raspy breath for what felt like forever, Autumn had no idea how long she'd been running. The shadows were lengthening, and the silence of the woods finally wrapped around her when she stopped again. The sounds of the fire that had been chasing her were gone and she could finally take a deep, shuddering breath.

The ground and all of the underbrush were wet. Even the air was damp, and she could feel the chill of the coming evening seeping in through her soggy clothes. Autumn knew that it couldn't be much later than four in the afternoon, but her limited outdoor experience made her aware that night came early in the mountains. What if she had to spend the night out there? How was she supposed to stay warm?

Wait!

Tilting her head to the side, much like a bird that is startled, she strained to hear a faint sound. Forcing herself to slow her breathing, she tried to concentrate.

There! It sounds like the freeway!

Her adrenaline once again surging, Autumn sprinted recklessly towards her possible salvation. Ignoring the steepening landscape, she slid down the muddy hillside, any rational thought gone for the moment. The journey came to an abrupt end when the ground disappeared beneath her, and she was suddenly nearly free falling down a cliff!

Landing hard on her backside, she put her hands and feet out to slow her descent. The pain of rocks slicing through her burns barely registered, and a part of her observed that she was almost numb to the ongoing agony.

Reaching the bottom of the ravine, Autumn discovered the source of what she thought was freeway noise: a small river. Screaming in frustration, she tried hard to fight back fresh tears.

Now what?

Looking around at her seemingly hopeless situation, Autumn recalled the survivalist shows she was forced to watch with her father.

"Follow the water downstream," she said aloud, her voice harsh. "It might ultimately lead to civilization." Staring at the water, she stood still in spite of her own encouraging words to move. It was flowing peacefully around her feet, and she wished it could wash away the terror that she knew was waiting to pounce. That…and panic. Plagued daily with anxiety, it was a constant battle for control.

Her feet were cold. Without really thinking about it, she began to trudge across to the other side, where there was enough room along the edge to walk on dry ground. Although she was feeling the first tug of thirst, she resisted the urge. One of the other lessons she learned from those TV shows, was that even though it looked like clean mountain water, it could be contaminated with microscopic organisms that would make her sick. Without a way to start a fire to boil it, drinking it was a risk. She decided to only drink it when she got really thirsty. She'd be okay for a day.

After going just a couple hundred feet, Autumn was

forced by rock outcroppings to cross back over to the other side. Although it hardly classified as a river, the water was deep enough, and the rocks slick enough, to pose a challenging obstacle course for the already battered teen. Her multiple burns, scratches, bruises, and abrasions were starting to hurt as the adrenaline wore off, making the journey even more difficult.

The terrain didn't relent, offering her no other choice than to continuously switch back and forth. She used fallen trees as bridges when possible, carefully picking her way through the branches that were still attached. When those weren't available, she tried to balance on the tops of the larger, exposed rocks, which resulted in multiple falls and several instances of being swept away briefly in the freezing cold water.

This went on for the rest of the long afternoon, until the setting sun and encroaching darkness forced Autumn out of her drone-like state. Looking up at the steep banks, she knew she needed to find a safe place to sleep. That wasn't possible down there in the water.

Her body aching beyond anything she'd ever experienced, Autumn scrambled painfully up the loose rocks and dirt. After backsliding a number of times, she finally reached the top, and then used the branches and underbrush to help pull her up to a flatter surface.

She eventually staggered into a small clearing, where the ground was littered with pine needles. It was likely the best spot she was going to find, and it was getting dark fast.

I have to get out of these wet clothes.

Drawing again from her meager survival knowledge, she stripped down to her underwear and tank top. Hanging the sopping clothes over nearby branches, she then wandered somewhat aimlessly, unsure of what to do next. Everything in those woods seemed wet. Even if she knew how to start a fire from scratch, there was no way she could find enough dry kindling to try it.

Now that she'd stopped moving, the aching in her joints intensified. The smallest of motions took an enormous amount of willpower and all Autumn wanted to do was sleep. To stop thinking and feeling. But it was so *cold*. Although they'd had record highs in that area over the past week, the temperature dropped about twenty degrees that weekend. It was probably still close to eighty that day at the lower elevations, but up there, she guessed it might be around fifty that night. After being in frigid water for hours, her clothes wet, and no way to warm up, hypothermia was a real concern.

Going to her clothes, she slowly picked up her brown cardigan. It was her favorite, and that small, familiar token brought her some comfort. Squeezing out as much water as she could, she then pulled it gingerly over her head, every burn screaming at the assault.

Circling the clearing, much like a dog in his kennel, she randomly picked out a spot and sat against a tree. Drawing her knees to her chest, she pulled the thick cardigan down over them as far as it would go, lowered her head, and breathed warm air into the small cocoon she'd created.

Now that she was away from the river, the silence

returned, enveloping her. It made her feel like a prisoner in her own mind, held in place by the empty air that had its own weight, pressing against her. It created too much opportunity to *think*. Unable to bear the prospect of a whole night alone out there in the dark woods, Autumn did the only thing she could think of to fill the void: sing.

She started with 'Sing Along,' by Karen O. The rhythmic, soothing melody instantly helped to calm her racing mind. As the night took over and darkness pressed in, she moved on to other familiar tunes. Crying and shivering, she prayed for the comforting bliss of a dreamless sleep.

2.The unforgiving terrain of The Northern Cascade Mountains, near Easy Pass.

3

Sunday, July 12, 2015

Time unknown

Something was moving nearby. The odd rustling sounds broke through Autumn's thin veil of sleep and she caught her breath, not daring to move. Was it a bear? A mountain lion?

Cautiously, she raised her head and was greeted with a dark so complete that she couldn't even see her knees that were just inches below her chin. Fear paralyzed her. Nighttime was always a challenge at home, and she would often call someone to talk with to help her fall asleep. This was literally one of her worst nightmares.

Maybe it'll just eat me, and we can get it over with.

She dismissed the thought quickly, wishing she could take it back and not tempt fate. Being eaten alive by some wild creature was *not* how she wanted to leave this world.

Whatever it was continued to sniff around and taunt her for the rest of the night. Mixed in with the distinct animal noises was something harder to describe. Whispers. Like a secret, hushed conversation heard from a distance, except that she could still hear it after plugging her ears. She must have nodded off at some point though, because she woke to the first blessed rays of sunshine on her face.

Eager to get moving and away from this place, she forced her stiff legs to unfold and used the tree to help her stand. Her right hand throbbed. Huge blisters covered it, and she whimpered at the pain that picking up her clothes caused. Once she got her damp jeans and mud-filled shoes on, Autumn lurched toward where she hoped the river was.

Wiping at her burning eyes with her left hand, she noticed an odd smell that had been trailing her since the day before. Mint. It was mixed in with the more subtle odor of pine needles and something else. Perhaps the rotting decay of the forest floor, or maybe it was the putrid flesh of her burned hand. Whatever it was, it didn't belong there. Nature was supposed to smell fresh and clean…not like that thick, cloying stench. Wrinkling her nose at it, Autumn did her best to ignore it, her paranoia suggesting that it represented something sinister.

It only took a few minutes to reach the river, and after a controlled slide, she fell back easily into the brain-numbing routine of the day before. Only this time, she started out already wet, cold, and hurting all over.

She didn't make it far before taking her first spill, the icy water swallowing her up, and spitting her back out a short distance downstream. Every time it happened, she had to painfully crawl to the shore and drag herself out. It was exhausting.

After about an hour, it got to the point where she was having a hard time catching her breath. She had never been diagnosed with asthma, but had always suspected that she might have it. Cold was one of the triggers for the slight constriction of her airway, and she couldn't stand the icy water any longer. When she saw two trees within easy reach, she made the decision to take a break.

Stripping again, Autumn lay down in between the evergreens and did her best to get warm. Or...maybe getting warm wasn't what she really wanted.

"I'm going to die," she said weakly at the empty forest. Maybe slipping off to sleep and succumbing to hypothermia wouldn't be all that bad.

"Please, just kill me! Make it fast," she added, praying to a God she hadn't spoken to in years, and wasn't even sure existed. This caused her to pause, and she reflected on the things she'd done in her life, both good and bad. People that she wished she could talk to one more time, to make things right. Her boyfriend.

Crying out, she begged for mercy. This couldn't happen...not like this. She wanted to feel a warm bed again, to go sit in a field with Newton and watch the sun set. To feel a hug again. What would happen to her...if she did die? She didn't know if there was a heaven.

What if I just ceased to exist?

This thought broke through the deep chill that had settled over her, and she pushed up on her forearms. What if no one found her body? If they did, what would it look like?

"I don't want to die out here alone," she sobbed, in total despair. "Help me! Please, God, someone help me."

A small, brown animal that looked like a giant gerbil peeked its head up nearby, and silently observed her. Watching it, Autumn decided to call it a forest gerbil, and smiled slightly as it scurried across the opening, just a few feet away. In the silence caused by the break in her crying, she heard something out of place.

"Is that a helicopter?" she gasped, nearly jumping to her feet. Spurred on by desperate hope, she propelled herself out of the space she thought would be her grave. But as soon as she walked to where there was a gap in the trees overhead, the sound was gone. Had it ever really been there?

While disappointed, she'd managed to recapture the motivation needed to continue. She refused to die out here.

3. The woods are thick in the mountains of the Pacific Northwest

4

The rest of the day turned into a blur of continuously crossing the river, which became deeper and swifter, and eventually lead to a large, twenty-foot waterfall. With no other options, Autumn had to pick her way down the rocks jutting out of it, adding to her cold and misery.

It ended up being the first of two waterfalls, but shortly after, the stream spread out to create more of a marsh. While it was less treacherous, trudging through the waist-deep muck was almost as bad.

She'd been forced to stop and rest several times already, her body quickly weakening. Thankfully, she drank some water while it was still flowing clean. Now, Autumn squinted at the lowering sun, dreading the possibility that it represented: spending another night out there.

Humming, she continued to distract herself with a broad spectrum of songs. It was the only thing that had kept her from going insane. She'd made it through nearly the whole song list from the movie Happy Feet, and was currently making the smacking sounds from Prince's song, Kiss.

Looking up to mark her progress, she paused.

Is that a trail?

The woods seemed to hold its breath in the silence as she made her way toward the flattened area ahead. Although hopeful, Autumn was reserved. Multiple times that day, she had been excited by what she thought was a sign of people and civilization, only to discover it was a trick of light or her imagination.

Sighing, she stepped out of the muck and onto something new: a sandbank. While relieved to finally reach level ground where she could walk on dry land, she couldn't help but be frustrated that it wasn't actually a trail.

Covered in thick, stinky mud, the exhausted teen began searching for a place to settle in until morning. As much as she wanted to deny it, night was once again winning the battle, and she hoped to be asleep before experiencing its full effects.

Preferring to have something at her back, Autumn selected a fallen log and then numbly went through the now familiar routine of stripping down and using her cardigan as a cover. At first, she was thankful for the soft, slightly warm padding that the sand provided. As the evening progressed though, it became clear that the location wasn't a good choice. Sand fleas emerged, and she could feel them crawling all over and biting her. Afraid to move blindly through the dark woods, she stayed put, and awoke to discover that a rash and countless bug bites were added to her injuries.

After taking stock of the multiple wounds, she longed to be the girl she was a mere forty-eight hours earlier. Everything had changed. While she wasn't sure if life could ever be the same again, she was eager to get home and appreciate what she had. Autumn did what seemed impossible, and stood up.

I didn't know that moving could hurt so bad.

Pushing herself, Autumn tried to ignore the pain. If she stopped moving, she'd never get out of there. No one would know what happened, or that her grandparents were dead.

Thinking of them caused a fresh round of sobs to break through, and Autumn almost missed the sound of a plane flying nearby. Tripping through the sand, she peered up through the trees, but didn't see anything.

Are they looking for me? she questioned, hope swelling in her chest. Wiping at her eyes, she moved to the next clearing and looked skyward. *Is it in the news? Are there search parties?*

Even though she couldn't see the plane, she was certain one was there. It wasn't like the helicopter or other things the day before, because this time it was obvious. Its engines faded away without any visual sign of it, but it was still encouraging.

It took a while to get moving, but she made slow progress walking along the bank. The marsh recollected itself into more of a defined creek, but the terrain remained level, so that she wasn't forced back into the water.

Once she was able to walk among the trees, she kept a close eye out for anything edible. She hadn't been hungry the past two days, but she woke up that morning with a gnawing ache in her stomach. However, nothing seemed to come easy there, and the only visible food was berries that weren't ripe enough to eat.

Unsure of how much time was passing, Autumn moved forward in a daze, remembering random things from her past and muttering the same songs from the day before.

When the sound of another plane approached, it barely broke through, jolting her to awareness. The tone was different. It was much closer. Pausing, the young girl watched in disbelief as the craft flew directly over! Screaming, waving her arms, Autumn willed the plane to turn around. They had to see her!

Running, she fell and then painfully pushed herself back up, flailing her weak arms at the retreating rescue party. "Come back!" she screamed, her voice sounding surreal. "Come back!" she repeated, unable to accept that they were leaving her. But they were. They didn't see her. Maybe no one would ever see her and she'd just slowly fade away like the plane.

Staring down at her hands in the dirt, Autumn realized that she'd fallen again, but hadn't gotten back up. What was the point?

Rising to her knees, she tried to take a breath and

found that it was getting more difficult again. In this vast space, it felt like the air was collapsing in on her, and she was slowly suffocating. She didn't know where she was. No one did.

Focusing on the deep ache in her right hand, the throbbing in her joints, and the raw burning wounds covering her body, she used it to prove to herself that she was still alive.

She stumbled to her feet.

"Just a little farther," she called to the forest gerbil she'd seen darting in and out of the trees throughout the morning. "We're going to make it."

This compelled her to dig deep into her memory for the songs from the movie, Over the Hedge. But she quickly gave up, deciding that she wasn't *that* far gone...yet.

Absently scanning the tree line for her furry friend, she noticed something that looked like a defined structure. Stopping, Autumn held a hand to shade her eyes. She had to be imagining things again. Just ahead, spanning the small river was a mystical-looking bridge made of logs. To either side of it, heading in opposite directions, was a well-defined, trampled down trail.

"It can't be real," she whispered, moving cautiously towards it, afraid that it would disappear if she went too fast. Reaching out, she reverently touched the smooth wood, and when it didn't fade away, sobbed with relief.

4. Looking down at Hwy 20 not far from Easy Pass

5

The bridge was real.

The trail was real too, and after a brief debate (and hugging the logs,) Autumn decided to continue her downward descent and took the path to the left.

It wound through the trees, painting a dreamlike, peaceful image that was in direct conflict to her current condition. Each step was more excruciating than the last, making this final trek feel like a test and rite of passage, having to prove that she was worthy of survival.

Finally, Autumn staggered into the trailhead parking lot. Looking around in wonder, she still didn't quite believe it was true. A large, wooden sign detailed the rules of the trail and she had to laugh at the name 'Easy Pass Trail.' There wasn't anything *easy* about it!

There was only one car parked in the lot, a small white sedan. Going to it, she found it empty, and decided to just wait for the owners to return, since she had no idea how far into the woods, or how remote the parking lot was. It didn't take long though before the fear that they might not come back wiggled its way into her thoughts. They could be on a long hiking trip. Someone might have even parked this car at the far end of a really long trail, and they wouldn't reach it for days.

Driven by her dread of the night, Autumn left the trailhead and followed the road, figuring that since it was the only way in and out, she wasn't likely to get lost. Fortunately, it turned out to be rather short, and met up with a large, well-used freeway.

This has to be highway twenty! Autumn thought, while approaching the thick, white fog line marking the edge. That was the road her grandparents were navigating by, and she knew that there should be a lot of traffic on it in the summer, as it led to several popular vacation destinations.

She made it! Choking around a sob of relief, Autumn resisted the temptation to just lie down right there. No one had seen her yet.

When the first car rapidly approached from the west, she looked up hopefully. Her legs threatened to buckle, but she willed herself to stay upright. As it came alongside her, she tentatively raised a dirty hand, and then watched in shock as it continued without even slowing down.

They didn't realize I need help, she scolded herself. *Why didn't I just flag them down?*

When the sound of the next car built, this time coming from the east, she was ready. Arms held high over her head, she shuffled right onto the white line and did her best to get their attention. But they didn't stop. Confused, she stepped back from the retreating vehicle. The driver had looked right at her.

Gazing down at her clothes, Autumn saw that she was a mess. She was covered in mud, and the parts of her skin that were still visible were battered with burns, cuts, and bruises. But couldn't they tell that she was just a desperate, young girl?

Moaning then, she did her best to rearrange the destroyed clothes and wipe the dirt from her face. This couldn't be happening.

More cars came into view, and in spite of her dramatic pleas, they each passed her by. When one of the occupants actually waved and smiled back, she lost it. Crying, almost hysterical, she jumped up and down, yelling at the smiling person, safe inside their car.

"Why are you doing this?" she wailed, as even more vacationers turned a blind eye to the frantic teen. "Do you know what I've been through?" Another driver made eye contact, but after waving her off, sped away without even tapping their brakes.

I'm going to die here.

Taking a step back from the traffic and the people who refused to help, Autumn didn't know what to do.

After surviving a plane crash and two days alone in the woods, I'm going to die on the side of this freaking highway!

Unable to stand the cold indifference any longer, she limped back down the road and into the parking lot. The white car was still there, and she stared at it for a bit, confused. A light rain began to fall, compelling her to seek shelter under the trailhead sign.

Gathering her legs to her chest, it was hard not to feel defeated. Why would no one help her? Before she could try to answer her own question, Autumn saw a flash of red enter the parking area, her vision blurred by the rain, or maybe from her tears. It was another car.

After coming to a stop, two men got out and they both looked in her direction. They obviously saw her, and they weren't going away. In fact, they were coming towards her.

"Oh God," she breathed, painfully getting to her feet. Were they real? Or was she imagining this, still curled up in a fetal position back in-between the two trees?

Longing more than ever to feel the hug of a loved one, Autumn Veatch took a step towards her rescuers. Crossing the small space that separated them, she remembered her grandparents, the wrecked plane, and the consuming fire. Fresh tears escaped, following the pathway of clean skin the previous ones created.

She could see the obvious look of concern on the men's faces then, and she knew that they wouldn't leave her. She wouldn't have to spend another night alone and afraid, her own fears and anxiety trying to envelope her.

"I need help," she finally managed to say to them, doing her best to appear strong. "I'm the only survivor of a plane crash."

The sound of her own voice admitting this finally drove home that this was real. All of it.

She was getting out alive.

The End

Authors note:

I want to thank Autumn Veatch for trusting me with her story. I need to make it clear, that while I wrote this, it *is* her story. This experience was shared with me during a nearly three-hour long interview, and was written with as much accurate detail as possible. It's been approved by Autumn and as such, she holds the copyright.

I was impressed with this young lady before I even had the honor of meeting her. After hearing her story first-hand, I can't express enough the strength and courage she has. Not only in what she endured during this harrowing experience, but also in how she handles the daily struggles of life. Autumn was very open with me in regards to her anxiety and related disorders. Like so many of us, she didn't realize how strong she was, until faced with a life-or-death situation. She hopes that by reaching out, she might be able to encourage others to have faith in themselves and realize their full potential.

We all have it within us to be survivors, whether it's from a plane crash in the middle of one of the most rugged wildernesses in America, or from a daily fight with our own demons. There is always something worth fighting for: yourself.

-Tara Ellis

PICTURES

5. The trailhead for Easy Pass Trail

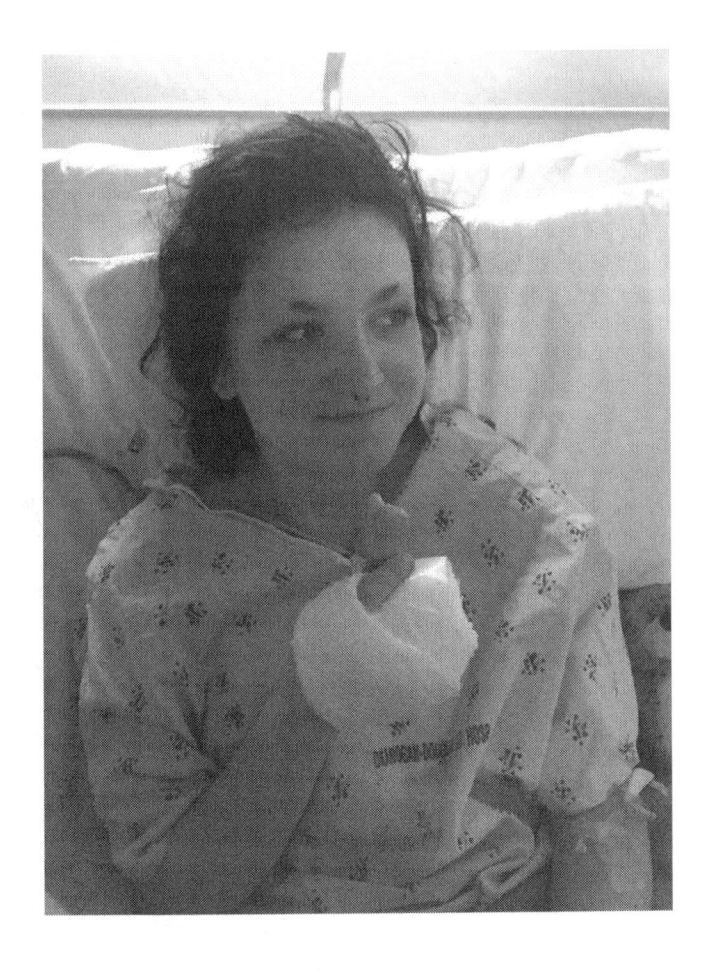

6. Autumn was treated for burns, dehydration, bruises, and abrasions.

7. Autumn was quickly reunited with family and friends and got those hugs!

If you enjoyed this short story, please consider leaving a review and checking out my full-length novels. You can find a completed, young adult trilogy, and an on-going middle grade mystery series here:

http://www.amazon.com/Tara-Ellis/e/B00IVF1JQK

You can sign up for my newsletter, and get notified of all new releases and specials!

eepurl.com/bzdHA5

ABOUT THE AUTHOR

Author Tara Ellis lives in a small town in beautiful Washington State, in the Pacific Northwest. She enjoys the quiet lifestyle with her husband, two teenage kids, and several dogs. Tara was a firefighter/EMT, and worked in the medical field for many years. She now teaches CPR, and concentrates on family, photography, and writing middle grade and young adult novels.

Visit her author page on Amazon to find all of her books!

Made in the USA
Charleston, SC
25 July 2016